OUR
GRE★T
STATES

WHAT'S GREAT ABOUT
WYOMING?

✳ Rebecca Felix

LERNER PUBLICATIONS ✳ MINNEAPOLIS

CONTENTS

Content Consultant: Tanis Lovercheck-
Saunders, PhD, History Department, Casper
College

Lerner Publications Company
A division of Lerner Publishing Group, Inc.
241 First Avenue North
Minneapolis, MN 55401 USA

For reading levels and more information, look
up this title at www.lernerbooks.com.

Main body text set in ITC Franklin Gothic Std
Book Condensed 12/15.
Typeface provided by Adobe Systems.

**Library of Congress Cataloging-in-Publication
Data**

Felix, Rebecca, 1984–
        What's great about Wyoming? / by
Rebecca Felix.
                pages   cm. — (Our great states)
        Includes index.
        Audience: Grades 4–6.
        ISBN 978-1-4677-3882-8 (lb : alk. paper)
        ISBN 978-1-4677-8521-1 (pb : alk. paper)
        ISBN 978-1-4677-8522-8 (EB pdf)
        1. Wyoming—Juvenile literature. I. Title.
F761.3.F43 2015
978.7—dc23   2015001953

Manufactured in the United States of America
1 – PC – 7/15/15

WYOMING Welcomes You!

Welcome to Wyoming! This land has rugged natural beauty and action-packed Wild West history. Hundreds of geysers and rushing rivers await you in the Cowboy State. Herds of bison and elk roam the plains, and ranchers rope and ride cattle and horses. Wyoming has fewer people than any other US state. But lots of visitors go to Wyoming each year looking for outdoor fun! You can dogsled through the Teton Mountains, ski snowy slopes, and dig for dinosaur bones. Read on to learn about what makes this state so great. Adventure awaits!

MONTANA

Yellowstone
National
Park

R O C K Y   M O U N T A I N S

Cody

Sheridan

BIGHORN MOUNTAINS

Bighorn River

Powder River

Gillette

Belle Fourche River

SOUTH DAKOTA

Grand Teton
National
Park

IDAHO

Jackson

Mount Gannett
(13,804 feet/
4,207 m)

Riverton

N

Miles
0   20   40   60
0   40   80
Kilometers

Casper

North Platte River

Green River

LARAMIE MOUNTAINS

NEBRASKA

Rock
Springs

G R E A T
D I V I D E
B A S I N

Medicine
Bow

Green River

Evanston

Laramie

Cheyenne

UTAH

COLORADO

Explore Wyoming's
wilderness and all the
places in between! Just
turn the page to find
out all about
THE COWBOY STATE. >

YELLOWSTONE
NATIONAL PARK

Buffalo are one of the many animals you may see while hiking at Yellowstone National Park.

> Have you ever seen a rainbow-colored pool? Or watched geysers shoot streams of water into the sky? You can see these incredible sights and many more at Yellowstone National Park. Mountains, forests, and hot springs are just some of its natural features.

Take ranger-guided hikes past hissing steam vents. Then step to the edge of deep blue sizzling springs ringed in yellowish sulfur deposits. Watch the park's most famous geyser, Old Faithful. It explodes every thirty minutes or so. Thousands of gallons of hot water shoot up for several minutes! The water goes between 130 and 140 feet (40 and 43 meters) high!

After the hike, explore the park's waterways on canoes or kayaks. You can also bike or hike the forests and fields full of wildlife. Or hitch a ride on a llama! You'll be assigned your very own llama on Yellowstone Safari Company's Llama Trek. Make friends with your furry guide as it carries you and your gear on an overnight adventure through the park.

GEYSERS

Yellowstone has about half of all the geysers in the world! Geysers form when magma heats water underground. The heated water creates pressure on the rocks around it. The pressure builds until the water explodes upward from the geyser. Sulfur left behind by the water creates colorful mounds. These mounds grow to look like familiar shapes. Geysers are sometimes named after these shapes. Yellowstone's Castle Geyser is one of these. It is one of three hundred geysers in the park.

CHEYENNE

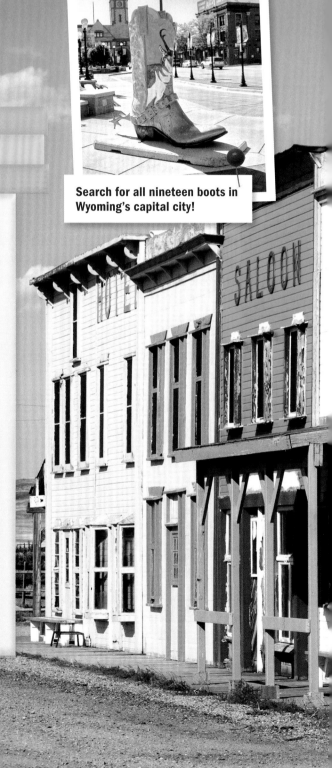

Search for all nineteen boots in Wyoming's capital city!

> You'll see cowboy boots twice your height all around Cheyenne. The boots are part of a citywide scavenger hunt. Each boot is painted differently. You can look for the boots from a horse-drawn carriage in the summer.

Next, hop on a train at Terry Bison Ranch outside of town. The ranch's trains run past a herd of bison. You'll also see ostriches and camels. Be sure to check out the pony rides and the Old West trading post before you leave the ranch.

Cheyenne has other Old West sights. See history in action at Gunslinger Square. Costumed cowboys act out skits and showdowns! You might even see one of the actors break out of jail during the show. Run around the stage after the show. Have your picture taken in front of the saloon or the jail.

TRANSCONTINENTAL RAILROAD

In the 1850s, thousands of people moved to the West Coast of the United States because of the gold rush. Many passed through Wyoming. The Union Pacific Railroad built tracks through Wyoming about fifteen years later. The tracks were part of a national project to connect the Union Pacific Railroad with the Central Pacific Railroad. Building this transcontinental railroad created jobs and brought more people to Wyoming. It also created the town of Cheyenne.

DOGSLEDDING

> Imagine sledding past snowy mountain peaks. Your sled twists and turns at top speed! But you're safe and sound under a cozy blanket. You have a front-row seat for the ultimate Wyoming winter adventure: dogsledding!

Riders of all ages can sled with Jackson Hole Iditarod Sled Dog Tours. Mushers train teams of huskies all year. Some teams and mushers travel to Alaska for the Iditarod, a yearly world-famous dogsled race. When home in Wyoming, the pups pull people through Bridger Teton National Forest.

Your next destination is Granite Hot Springs in Jackson. In the winter, you can reach the springs only by snowmobile, snowshoe, or dogsled. Hop right into the steaming water! The hot springs are like natural hot tubs. You'll be warm even when there's snow all around!

Warm up at Granite Hot Springs.

Meet the sled dogs when you stop for hot drinks and soup.

DINOSAUR AND FOSSIL ADVENTURES

> Did you know dinosaurs once roamed Wyoming's plains? Or that part of the state was once underwater? It's true! Fossil evidence tells us that millions of years ago, Wyoming was wet and warm year-round. Thousands of fossils of ancient fish, bugs, crocodiles, and other animals are found at Fossil Butte National Monument each year. Maybe you'll spot some on your visit! Sign up for the Fossil Quarry Program if you visit on a summer weekend. You can help hunt for fossils at a real dig site.

More ancient fun awaits at the Wyoming Dinosaur Center. At least ten thousand fossilized bones have been found nearby. Help unearth some as part of the Dig for a Day program. It is offered during spring, summer, and fall. Head into the center's museum next. There you can check out full dinosaur skeletons. One is from a huge *Supersaurus* named Jimbo. There are also *Tyrannosaurus rex* and triceratops skeletons on display. The triceratops is Wyoming's state dinosaur.

How many fossils can you spot at Fossil Butte National Monument?

WYOMING DINOSAURS

In 1877, railroad employees spotted big bones sticking out of the ground near Medicine Bow. Thousands of fossils have been discovered in the state since then. Many fossils found in Wyoming are well preserved. Water and lake sediments kept these fossils in place. Wyoming's fossils help scientists better understand what life was like when dinosaurs roamed Earth.

13

Try fly-fishing in the Little Laramie River near the Vee Bar Guest Ranch.

DUDE RANCHES

> Want to ride Wyoming trails on horseback? Would you like to sit around a cowboy campfire and share tales? Then a Wyoming dude ranch is for you!

Horseback riding is the main focus at Lazy L&B Ranch in Dubois. But there are lots of other activities. Breakfast is cooked over a campfire. Then you'll help cowboys groom and saddle the horse that you'll ride all week. The river is perfect for swimming after a hot day on the trail. There's even a petting zoo! And don't miss the kids-only cookout campfire.

The Vee Bar Guest Ranch in Laramie offers fishing lessons. Squeeze in a session between horseback trail rides, hayrides, and river tubing trips. You can learn to herd sheep with a real wrangler. Then get ready for a branding session! Bring your own leather wallet, belt, boots, or hat. Stamp them with a sizzling-hot iron to make a wearable memory of your wild Wyoming adventure.

Enjoy breakfast that has been cooked over the fire at Lazy L&B Ranch.

JACKSON HOLE

> The steep peaks surrounding Jackson Hole are covered in deep snow in the winter. This makes the mountains perfect for skiing. People visit the area from around the world to take part in winter sports.

Are you new to snowboarding? Have you ever raced down a snowy mountain on skis? Jackson Hole Mountain Resort has you covered, no matter your skill level. Take lessons at their Kids Ranch Ski School. Beginners will learn to tackle the towering terrain. Or challenge yourself to a mountain racecourse if you have more experience.

There's no need to race when you're exploring Jackson Hole on snowshoes. Take the Hole Hiking Experience's snowshoeing and sleigh-ride adventure. You will snowshoe through Grand Teton National Park. Then ride a horse-drawn sleigh through the National Elk Refuge. You might run through a herd of hundreds of elk!

Take the Jackson Hole aerial tram to try to spot elk from the air in the summer. The tram takes you to the top of Jackson Hole. Kids who weigh 40 pounds (18 kilograms) or more can coast down the mountainside with Jackson Hole Paragliding's pros by their side.

Which wild animals will you see from Jackson Hole's aerial tram?

With practice, you can tackle the black diamond ski runs.

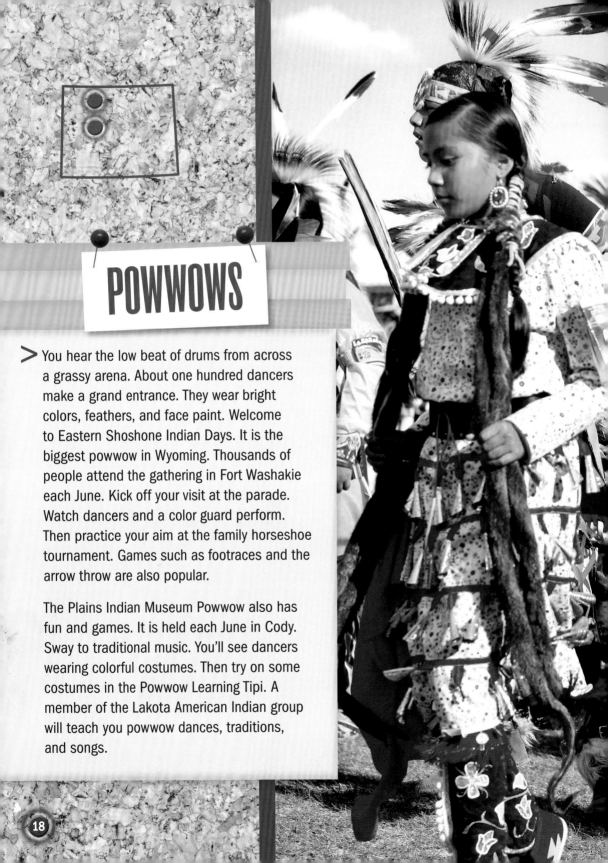

POWWOWS

> You hear the low beat of drums from across a grassy arena. About one hundred dancers make a grand entrance. They wear bright colors, feathers, and face paint. Welcome to Eastern Shoshone Indian Days. It is the biggest powwow in Wyoming. Thousands of people attend the gathering in Fort Washakie each June. Kick off your visit at the parade. Watch dancers and a color guard perform. Then practice your aim at the family horseshoe tournament. Games such as footraces and the arrow throw are also popular.

The Plains Indian Museum Powwow also has fun and games. It is held each June in Cody. Sway to traditional music. You'll see dancers wearing colorful costumes. Then try on some costumes in the Powwow Learning Tipi. A member of the Lakota American Indian group will teach you powwow dances, traditions, and songs.

Plains Indians use traditional drums to beat out rhythms at their powwows in Cody.

THE PURPOSE OF POWWOWS

Wyoming is home to many American Indian peoples. These include the Arapaho, the Crow, the Lakota, and the Shoshone, among others. Many groups hold powwows to express and celebrate their culture. These gatherings help keep traditions alive. Powwows can be uplifting. Tribal members have said that powwows help inspire and heal people who are sick or sad.

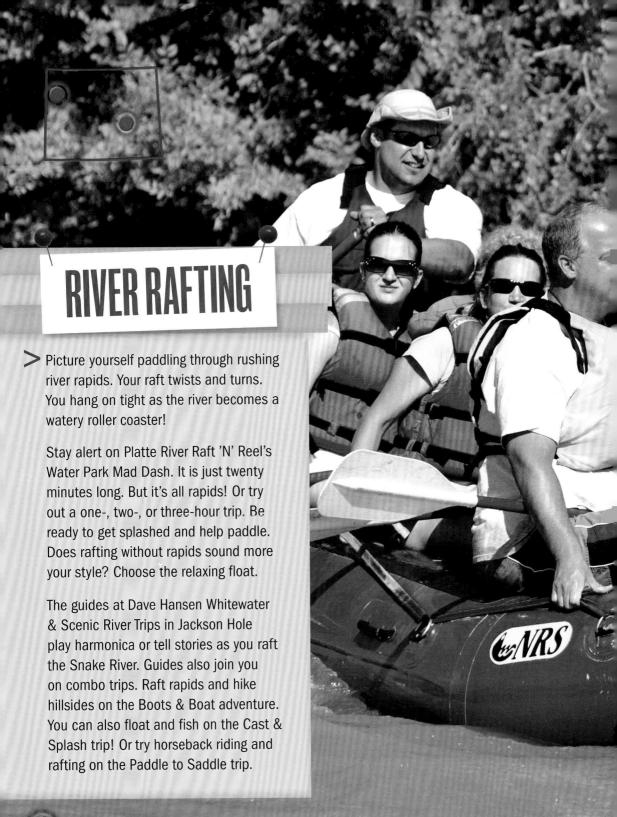

RIVER RAFTING

> Picture yourself paddling through rushing river rapids. Your raft twists and turns. You hang on tight as the river becomes a watery roller coaster!

Stay alert on Platte River Raft 'N' Reel's Water Park Mad Dash. It is just twenty minutes long. But it's all rapids! Or try out a one-, two-, or three-hour trip. Be ready to get splashed and help paddle. Does rafting without rapids sound more your style? Choose the relaxing float.

The guides at Dave Hansen Whitewater & Scenic River Trips in Jackson Hole play harmonica or tell stories as you raft the Snake River. Guides also join you on combo trips. Raft rapids and hike hillsides on the Boots & Boat adventure. You can also float and fish on the Cast & Splash trip! Or try horseback riding and rafting on the Paddle to Saddle trip.

Ride horseback after rafting on the Paddle to Saddle trip.

How many fish can you catch on the Cast & Splash trip?

CASPER

> Make Casper your next stop. Here you can learn more about science. Or you can stand in the spot where a historic battle took place. There's also an art museum where you can bring your imagination to life!

US soldiers and American Indians battled long ago at Casper's trading post and mail station. This area is called the Fort Caspar Museum in modern times. You'll see actors in costumes reenact battles from the past.

Next, stop by the Science Zone to see live animals. Take the whole day to explore its many exhibits. One Friday each month is Night at the Museum. You'll get to stay overnight! The event includes a tour and a movie you watch from your sleeping bag. The Casper Planetarium shows space-themed movies. It also offers telescopes for star sightings and the chance to build your own rocket!

Create anything you can dream up at the Nicolaysen Art Museum. This museum has a lot of modern art. Paint, magnets, and Lego bricks are just some of the materials you can use in its Discovery Center. What will you create?

Look for the bearded dragon
at the Science Zone.

See vintage tools and weapons on
display at the Fort Caspar Museum.

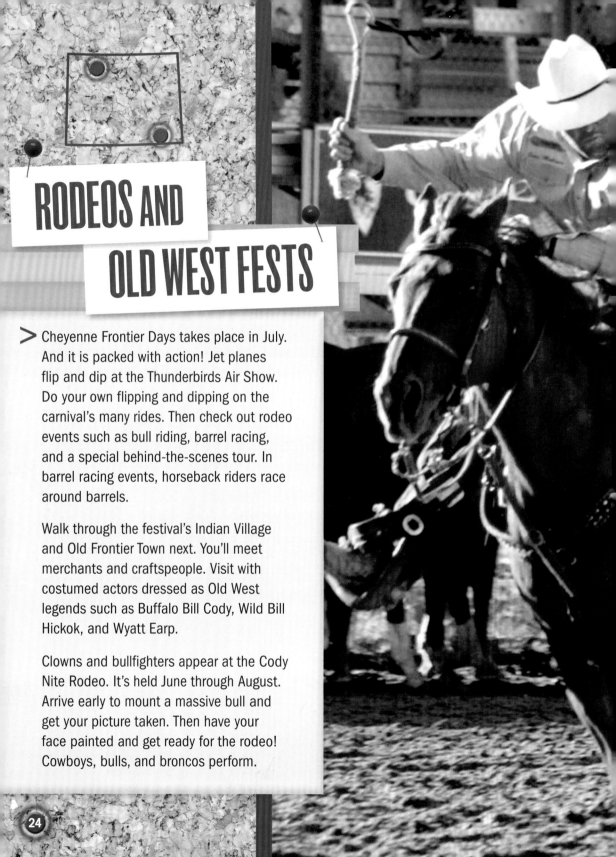

RODEOS AND OLD WEST FESTS

> Cheyenne Frontier Days takes place in July. And it is packed with action! Jet planes flip and dip at the Thunderbirds Air Show. Do your own flipping and dipping on the carnival's many rides. Then check out rodeo events such as bull riding, barrel racing, and a special behind-the-scenes tour. In barrel racing events, horseback riders race around barrels.

Walk through the festival's Indian Village and Old Frontier Town next. You'll meet merchants and craftspeople. Visit with costumed actors dressed as Old West legends such as Buffalo Bill Cody, Wild Bill Hickok, and Wyatt Earp.

Clowns and bullfighters appear at the Cody Nite Rodeo. It's held June through August. Arrive early to mount a massive bull and get your picture taken. Then have your face painted and get ready for the rodeo! Cowboys, bulls, and broncos perform.

See clowns perform at the Cody Nite Rodeo.

American Indian dance performances are just one of the exciting events at Cheyenne Frontier Days.

YOUR TOP TEN!

You've just read about ten things that make Wyoming great. What sounded like the most fun to you? Imagine you're planning a Wyoming trip. What places or activities would you include? Turn a list of your top ten choices into a book just like this one! Draw pictures of the activities you chose. Or search in magazines and online for images. Have fun dreaming up your own Wyoming top ten!

WYOMING BY MAP

> MAP KEY

- Capital city
- City
- Point of interest
- Highest elevation
- State border

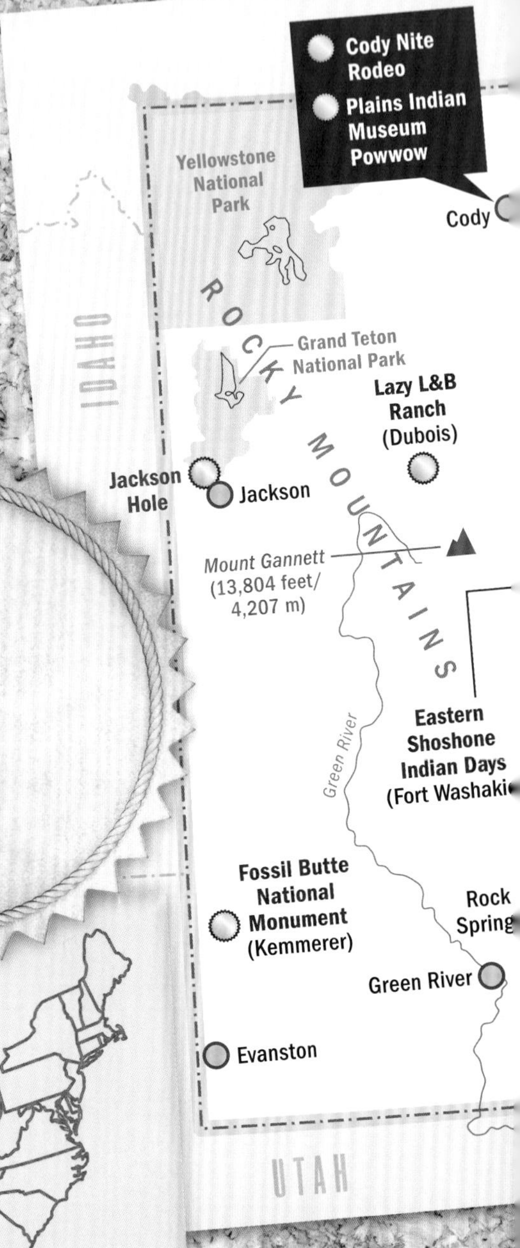

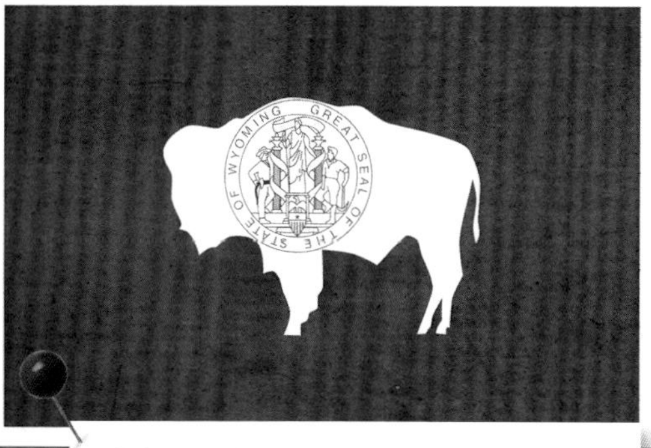

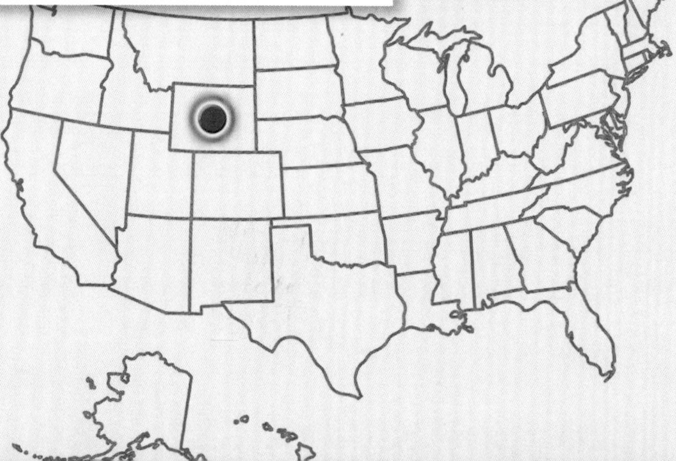

Cody Nite Rodeo
Plains Indian Museum Powwow
Cody
Yellowstone National Park
ROCKY MOUNTAINS
IDAHO
Grand Teton National Park
Lazy L&B Ranch (Dubois)
Jackson Hole
Jackson
Mount Gannett (13,804 feet/ 4,207 m)
Green River
Eastern Shoshone Indian Days (Fort Washaki
Fossil Butte National Monument (Kemmerer)
Rock Spring
Green River
Evanston
UTAH

GREAT SEAL OF THE STATE OF WYOMING

Visit www.lerneresource.com to learn more about the state flag of Wyoming.

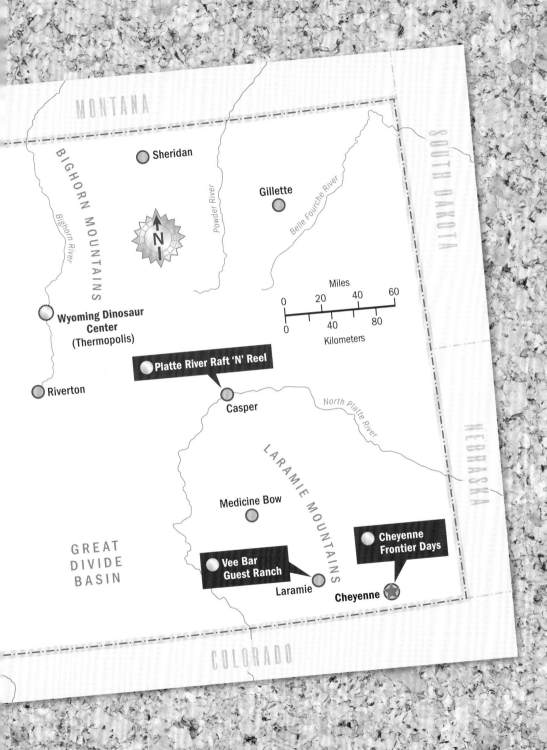

MONTANA

SOUTH DAKOTA

Sheridan

Gillette

Powder River

Belle Fourche River

BIGHORN MOUNTAINS

Bighorn River

N

Miles
0   20   40   60

0   40   80
Kilometers

Wyoming Dinosaur
Center
(Thermopolis)

Riverton

Platte River Raft 'N' Reel

Casper

North Platte River

NEBRASKA

LARAMIE MOUNTAINS

GREAT
DIVIDE
BASIN

Medicine Bow

Cheyenne
Frontier Days

Vee Bar
Guest Ranch

Laramie

Cheyenne

COLORADO

WYOMING FACTS

NICKNAME: The Cowboy State; The Equality State; Big Wyoming

SONG: "Wyoming" by Charles E. Winter

MOTTO: Equal Rights

FLOWER: Wyoming Indian paintbrush

TREE: cottonwood

BIRD: meadowlark

DATE AND RANK OF STATEHOOD: July 10, 1890; the 44th state

CAPITAL: Cheyenne

AREA: 97,914 square miles (253,596 sq. km)

AVERAGE JANUARY TEMPERATURE: 19°F (-7°C)

AVERAGE JULY TEMPERATURE: 67°F (19°C)

POPULATION AND RANK: 582,658; 50th (2013)

MAJOR CITIES AND POPULATIONS: Cheyenne (62,448), Casper (59,628), Laramie (31,814), Gillette (31,797), Rock Springs (24,138)

NUMBER OF US CONGRESS MEMBERS: 1 representative, 2 senators

NUMBER OF ELECTORAL VOTES: 3

NATURAL RESOURCES: clay, coal, petroleum, soil

AGRICULTURAL PRODUCTS: beef cattle, corn, hay, hogs, wheat

MANUFACTURED GOODS: chemicals, machinery, metal products, petroleum products

STATE HOLIDAYS AND CELEBRATIONS: Wyoming State Fair and Rodeo

GLOSSARY

aerial tram: a vehicle that runs on high cables or rails

branding: making a burn mark on something to show ownership

geyser: an underground hot spring that blasts hot water and steam into the air

magma: melted underground rock

musher: a person who drives dogsleds

paragliding: a sport in which people jump from a high place and float to the ground using a special parachute

powwow: an American Indian social gathering that usually involves music and dancing

rapid: a spot in a river where water flows very fast

sulfur: a yellowish, nonmetallic chemical

tipi: a tentlike dwelling used by some American Indians

LERNER

SOURCE™

Expand learning beyond the printed book. Download free, complementary educational resources for this book from our website, www.lerneresource.com.

FURTHER INFORMATION

Byers, Ann. *Wyoming: Past and Present*. New York: Rosen Central, 2011. Read about Wyoming's natural beauty and natural resources and how the history of its people and settlement shaped the state today.

Explore the States: Wyoming
http://www.americaslibrary.gov/es/wy/es_wy_subj.html
Check out photos and learn more about Wyoming cowboys and American Indians, Yellowstone, and the history of Cheyenne Frontier Days.

Figley, Marty Rhodes. *Clara Morgan and the Oregon Trail Journey.* Minneapolis: Millbrook Press, 2011. Learn about a family's journey through Wyoming.

***National Geographic*: Yellowstone**
http://www.nationalgeographic.com/features/97/yellowstone
Watch a video of a geyser explode and hear the sound it makes. You can also hear the sounds made by mud pots, hot springs, steam vents, and other Yellowstone thermal features.

Prentzas, G. S. *Wyoming*. New York: Children's Press, 2010. Find fun facts, photos, and more information on Wyoming's land, people, animals, history, and government.

Wyoming for Kids
http://www.wyoming4kids.org
Play games, watch videos, check out photos, and take fun quizzes about Wyoming's animals, land, history, fossils, and more.

INDEX

PHOTO ACKNOWLEDGMENTS

The images in this book are used with the permission of: © Sam Strickler/Shutterstock Images, p. 1; NASA, pp. 2–3; © Laura Westlund/Independent Picture Service, pp. 5 (top), 27; © dszc/iStockphoto, p. 5 (bottom); © American Spirit/Shutterstock Images, p. 4; Jim Peaco/National Park Service, pp. 6, 6–7; © Capture Light/Shutterstock Images, p. 7; © www.CGPGrey.com CC 2.0, pp. 8–9; © Cliff CC 2.0, p. 8; Ed Anderson/Library of Congress, p. 9 (HAER CAL,31-CISCO,4—2); © Bridget Clyde/StockShot/Alamy, pp. 10–11; © Stephanie Graeler/Alamy, p. 11 (right); © pychap CC 2.0, p. 11 (left); © Ben Townsend CC 2.0, pp. 12–13; National Park Service, p. 12; © James St. John CC 2.0, p. 13; © whatleydude CC 2.0, pp. 14–15; © Tony Campbell/Shutterstock Images, p. 14; © Delmas Lehman/Shutterstock Images, p. 15; Lori Iverson/US Fish and Wildlife Service, pp. 16–17; © m01229 CC 2.0, p. 17 (left); © H. Mark Weidman Photography/Alamy, p. 17 (right); © Luc Novovitch/Alamy, pp. 18–19; © Lee Foster/Alamy, p. 19 (top); US Army Signal Corps, p. 19 (bottom); © Andrew Woodley/Alamy, pp. 20–21, 25 (left); © bikeriderlondon/Shutterstock Images, p. 21 (bottom); © Dragon Images/Shutterstock Images, p. 21 (top); © Greg Ryan/Alamy, pp. 22–23; © KobchaiMa/Shutterstock Images, p. 23 (top); © Dan Cepeda/The Tyler Morning Telegraph/AP Images, p. 23 (bottom); © Larry Jacobsen CC 2.0, pp. 24–25; © Lincoln Rogers/Shutterstock Images, p. 25 (right); © nicoolay/iStockphoto, p. 26; © Julius Fekete/Shutterstock Images, p. 29 (top); © Tom Reichner/Shutterstock Images, p. 29 (middle left); Carol M. Highsmith/Library of Congress, p. 29 (middle right) (LC-DIG-highsm-16996); © Michal Madacky/Shutterstock Images, p. 29 (bottom).

Front cover: © Education Images/UIG via Getty Images (Jackson Hole); © Oscarcwilliams/Dreamstime.com (boot sculpture); © Lane V. Erickson/Shutterstock.com (Yellowstone National Park); © Bdingman/Dreamstime.com (Cheyenne Frontier Days Powwow); © Laura Westlund/Independent Picture Service (map); © iStockphoto.com/fpm (seal); © iStockphoto.com/vicm (pushpins); © iStockphoto.com/benz190 (corkboard).